My Journey
to a
New World

A MEMOIR

BITISHO MAWAZO

For more information, visit: http://www.myjourneytoanewworld.com/

ISBN: 979-8-218-42430-5 (paperback)
ISBN: 979-8-218-42790-0 (eBook)

Cover Design by Kelly Nielsen, Studio 92
Book Interior and E-book Design by Amit Dey

DEDICATION

To my lovely husband, Mathias

To our children Harley and Melissa,
and our niece Cheka

To my parents, Uzia and Mashango

To my sisters and brothers

TABLE OF CONTENTS

CHAPTER 1: My Childhood 1

CHAPTER 2: Getting Married 7

CHAPTER 3: The War – Had to Flee 17

CHAPTER 4: Why California? 27

CHAPTER 5: Life in Oakland. 75

CHAPTER 6: The Kids 83

CHAPTER 7: My Career Path. 91

CHAPTER 8: Becoming a U.S. Citizen 101

CHAPTER 9: Ups and Downs of Marriage 113

CHAPTER 10: What the Future Holds 121

About the Author 127

MY CHILDHOOD

B orn in the country known as the Democratic Republic of Congo, specifically the region of South Kivu, city of Uvira, in 1972, I grew up in a polygamist family. Since my dad came from a polygamist family, he was totally comfortable having six wives; however, my mom was his first wife. The sixth child of my parents' children included two girls and four boys; when my mom was pregnant with me, my dad hit her in the stomach, and as a result, her pregnancy was almost aborted. They had to rush my mom to the hospital in order to save me as a baby.

After examining her, the doctor said, "You have two options. You can have an abortion as it is early enough, and we don't know if there is any long-term damage to the baby or you can keep it, but you will have to stay in the hospital for six months."

Only three months pregnant then, my mom wanted to have a girl because she already had four boys, though my dad thought she should have an abortion. Even though she knew it would be hard, somehow, she knew I would be a girl and chose to stay in the hospital before having a C-section. My Mom named me "Bitisho" which means 'surprise.'

After hearing what my mom went through, I totally understand the situation now because she was in pretty bad shape. Seeing her go through all that pain and suffering was hard for my dad. He felt a little bit guilty because he wanted my mom to be alive. She said to him, "It could be a baby girl." I empathize with both sides now because when my brother was six months old, she was three months pregnant with me. So, that put a lot of pressure on both of them. While it would have been easier to have an abortion, she couldn't do it, so here I am.

My Dad wanted a baby girl, too, and I turned out to be his favorite. My last name, Mawazo, is my Grandma's name on my Dad's side. In our culture, one child has to have the Grandmother's name, so when she passes, it replaces her name. My Dad calls me Mom because I have his Mom's name. I feel honored because everyone in my family has my Dad's last name, except me, since I have my Grandma's name.

While I realize that domestic violence occurs everywhere, and nowadays, there are laws to help protect women, back then, in our world, it was accepted. Polygamy is common in the Democratic Republic of Congo, and traditionally, most African societies have practiced a custom of polygamy. This custom allows a man to have as many wives as he can support. Such a practice was not considered evil or immoral/sinful until the Christian missionaries arrived in Africa.

The main purpose of polygamy in a religious group is to be able to have more children, and that means the man and his wives are expected to continue to procreate as much as possible. Polygamy has several economic, social, and health advantages over monogamy. In most African cultures, women contribute significantly to the wealth of the household and can then materially benefit from the labor of an additional spouse.

A marriage certificate might sound like just a piece of paper, but for the women who live there, it is an important step towards greater security, self-reliance, and securing rights. Men can take multiple wives and since my Dad was quite wealthy, women flocked to him like bees to honey. As long as a man can feed and care for them, it is totally legal. If a man can't support them or doesn't love them, then they can leave. He was definitely looked upon as a macho man.

Our lifestyle was considered normal to me, and I didn't see any problem with it because that is how I grew up. Our family had twenty-two kids, and we all grew up together. As you can imagine, there was always someone to play with that many children. We never called each other half-brother or half-sister because we all belonged to my dad, and it was quite fun growing up with so many siblings. There was never a dull moment.

They had a scheduled system where my dad would be with one wife for 3-4 days and stay with her in her room for that time. Then, he would move on to another wife and stay with her for 3-4 days. Whichever wife my dad was sleeping with, she was in charge of the household, especially the kitchen, where the other wives would help her with all the food preparation. When my dad would move on to sleep with another wife, she would be in charge. Even though we had maids, the other wives were still expected to help care for us all. My Dad built a big enough house where each wife had their own bedroom. Another house was built in the backyard that was like a small apartment for all of us kids.

As you can imagine, mealtimes were like a banquet each day, feeding many children and adults. Breakfast would consist of eggs, bread, and tea, or some days, we would have oatmeal or porridge. As soon as we finished breakfast, we had to start preparing for lunch, typically dinner, meaning we ate our largest meal of the day at noon. Cooking started at 5 am so it would be ready on time.

Most of the time, we cooked bread over the stove made from Cassava flour from Cassava roots. In French, it means "manioc" because the roots grow like potatoes under the ground, and we would also eat the Cassava leaves. We prepared them much like you would prepare mashed potatoes. We boiled water, added the flour to the water, and then started mashing it like mashed potatoes. It would be like cooked dough that we ate with meat, fish, and vegetables. In the tropical area where we lived, that is the main meal in that area. We would have beans with rice or potatoes for dinner, and sometimes meat with plantains. Growing up with twenty-two kids, my siblings and I are the oldest kids from my mom and dad. My dad's second wife came after I was two years old, so everyone else was younger than us.

Located two blocks from our house, I went to a Catholic elementary school called Tanganyika Elementary School for first to sixth grade. I was in a car accident when I was around ten years old. My Dad had a store selling clothing and electronics, such as radios and televisions. My Mom would sometimes help him with selling items. One week, I would go to school from 7 am until 12 noon, and the other week, I would go from 12:30 to 5:30 pm. We would attend school one week in the morning and one week in the afternoon. My mom would have to make our lunch before we went to school, but I couldn't find her and thought she had gone to the store.

That day, around 11 Am., I went out to find her so she could make our lunch before heading off to school. When crossing the road, I didn't see the Jeep heading right toward me, and it ran me over. Lying down in the middle of the road, the people who saw what happened thought I was dead. The driver was so scared that he took off thinking he had killed me and thought other people who saw what happened would kill him, too. Fortunately, the people came to my aid, put me in a taxi, and sent me to the hospital.

Immediately, someone went and told my parents about the accident, and I soon realized I was okay with only a bruise on one knee. Those who saw the accident described the car and driver to my dad, who went on a search to find the man who hit me. After driving 60 miles from where the accident had occurred, he found him, and it turned out to be the manager of our local bank and his best friend. My dad was a customer, and they knew each other quite well.

When my Dad found him, he said to him, "It is okay – my daughter is fine – she didn't die."

He looked at my dad in shock, "I didn't know that was your daughter."

"Don't worry, she is doing fine," my dad said to him in a reassuring tone.

From that day on, my dad sternly told me, "Don't go out looking for your Mom. Stay home and wait for her to come back."

Two years later, I was in 6th grade, and that summer, I went to see my sister to spend the summer with her. Married and living in a town next to ours called Sange, we enjoyed the long, hot summers together. When it was time to go home, we left in the car, and I was in my second car accident when the tire exploded on the driver's side, causing the vehicle to roll over and the driver to die. All I remember was the car flipped repeatedly, but I came out of it okay with nothing but a bump on my forehead. Other people were injured, but I lost only my boots.

"I loved those boots," I remember saying to my sister.

She replied, rather annoyed, "Be thankful you are alive. Quit worrying about your boots."

After 6th grade, it was time for me to go to high school, where we start from the beginning, meaning 1st and 2nd grade are considered middle school, while 3rd – 6th grade is high school. Once you reach 3rd grade, you have to choose what you want to do in your life. We had so many programs to choose from, including math, physics, technology, and science, but I chose to be a teacher, known as Pedagogy, which means teaching. The nuns managed the all-girl school for teachers called Lycée Umoja High School. In 1994, I was excited to receive my high school diploma, ready to take on the world as a teacher.

GETTING MARRIED

I met my boyfriend, now my husband, who went to the same school as my two older brothers, so he knew them both well. In my younger years, I recall him coming to our home one day, but I was a little girl at the time. He went to the university to earn his bachelor's degree when he graduated high school. By this time, it was September of 1991, and he came home because someone told him that I was all grown up and could date me. Actually, he saw my picture in his nephew's photo album and told him he was a friend of my brothers.

When he saw my picture, he asked his nephew, "Who is that?"

"That is Bitisho," he told him.

"Wow – she is all grown up," he said with a feeling of excitement.

At the time, he was in his last year of getting his bachelor's degree, and before he came home, he gave a letter to his nephew to give to me. The letter said, "I am coming home for the summer and would like to meet you."

When he came to the house, my family thought he was coming to see my brothers, but instead, he asked, "Where is Bitisho?"

They told him, "She is not home – she is at our neighbor's house."

When I finally came home, I found him and my two brothers, and he said to me, "I came to see you. I saw your picture and would like to get to know you. Can we be friends?"

"Yes," I replied, surprised by his interest.

He came up and whispered in my ear, "Meet me at the beach tomorrow afternoon."

"Okay," I replied, excited to have a secret rendezvous with him.

His name was Mathias, and the next day, we met on the beach and were finally alone together. He started sharing with me why he was interested in me. At first, he was glad to hear that I was going to school to become a teacher, but then he went on and said how much he liked my eyes and smile.

"Are you really serious?" I asked him.

"Yes," he replied, holding my hand.

Even though I was sixteen and very young and underage, I knew he was the one for me. To be honest, most of the guys at the university approach women just to play with them, not to marry them. A friend had a guy tell her he would marry her, but he didn't mean it. He would do that so the family would give him everything and get what he wanted.

While I thought he was sincere, I said to him, "I don't want you to tell me that you want to marry me and then not do it."

"I am at the end of my education, and when I am finished, I want to come home and marry you," he replied with a loving look.

I smiled at him and said, "Okay."

After one week, he came back to our home again, and by that time, I knew he had come for me. My family kept thinking he was coming to see my brothers, not me. We were cooking dinner when one of my brothers started saying, "This is not right; why is he with my sister?"

My brother, Jonathan, warned Mathias, saying, "If you are not coming to see us, then you are not needed here. We don't understand you now and don't want to see you here."

"Why?" Mathias asked.

"You need to leave," Jonathan said, pointing to the door.

I told Mathias, "Stay here," and went to find my Dad, who was watching TV at the time. He would tell me if he didn't want Mathias there, but he didn't realize what was going on until he found out he was coming there for me.

"Just leave," Jonathan repeated.

"I will go with you," I said. "They are just jealous. It will be okay."

When I came back to the house, everything was fine. I expected my Dad to be upset, but all my parents knew was that Mathias was coming back for me. Eventually, my family was all okay with it because all I could think was that it wasn't my problem - it was their problem.

After that summer, Mathias went back to finish his education in Business Management at the University of Cepromad in Lubumbashi, which is located in the Southeast area of Congo. We managed to maintain a long-distance relationship, sending each other letters to stay in touch. In 1993, he graduated and came home, while I still had one year of high school to finish. That didn't stop us, as that was the year we got engaged.

When my Dad realized that Mathias wanted to marry me, he refused to accept the idea because he didn't want me to be married. He wanted me to go to university. Even after I shared with my brothers and Mom that when I was with Mathias, he was such a loving man who truly cared about me, they didn't want to hear it and didn't accept him.

"Why do you want to be married?" my Dad asked. "Why don't you want to go to University?"

"I love him," I replied emphatically. "I want to be married to him."

"Okay," my Dad relented. "We will call the whole family together and take a vote on whether they want you to be married."

Everyone said, "No."

That night, I went back into my room and started crying. I didn't wake up to go to school and remained in my room for two days.

My mom told my dad, "She didn't go to school."

My Dad said, "If she wants to kill herself, she can do that, but I don't want her to be married, period."

After two days, my sister-in-law, Justin's wife, came to my bedroom window and started knocking, saying, "Bitisho, no one wants you to be married. We just want you to be alive—are you still alive?"

Around 9 pm., I opened my window teary-eyed and said, "I am alive."

"It will be okay," she said in a reassuring tone.

Since I didn't go to school for two days, my teachers and friends wanted to know what happened to me. As you can imagine, the rumors were flying around in the community that my parents didn't want me to be married.

In the end, people knew I was very serious and started telling my dad, "If she loves him, let her be married. She could be pregnant – let her be pregnant."

"I just don't want her to be married," he insisted.

The next day, I went to school and told my friend the whole story. She said, "You know what? You can go to an older person that your dad respects."

"I know who we can go see," I replied. "My dad's older brother – my uncle."

After school, my friend and I went to see my uncle, and when I told him the story, he asked us, "Why?"

When we told him what my Dad kept saying, he said, "I know Mathias – I don't understand – he is a good guy. Why doesn't he want you to marry?"

"He wants me to go to school," I replied.

My uncle said he would see what he could do for me, talk to my Dad, and share his knowledge of Mathias' good character. We thanked him and left.

As a teenager, it felt like no one understood me at home. Eventually, my Dad gave in, mainly because people in town bombarded him and, frankly, was embarrassed. He was tired of hearing about it and was forced to accept Mathias so we could get married. One day, he called me, my mom, and my brother Justin and asked me again, "Why do you want to be married?"

"I love him – I feel like he is the perfect person for me," I insisted.

He said, "Well, if he really loves you, he should wait for you to finish school."

"Yes – I understand that – but he would let me go to school after we are married," I explained.

"When you are married, you will start having kids, and it will be hard for you to go back to school," my Dad remarked right back.

"I know," I said, "Mathias went to university and has a bachelor's degree so he knows the value of education."

When I told him that, I could see it in his eyes, he was defeated. When Mathias came over, I finally told him, "My parents respect you, and you need to present yourself to my family so we can get married."

Mathias went and told his family that he had a future wife and now wanted to come and make it official. That is how we got engaged. Then his family sent two people, his older brother, and his sister's husband, and told my family that Mathias' family was coming to make it official, but not Mathias—only his two family members.

When we knew they were coming to our home, we made a huge meal for our new visitors, placing all the food on the table. After eating, they said to my mom, dad and family, "Our son, Mathias, told us that he found a future wife in this family."

Even though my dad thought I was too young to be married, he asked, "Which one is that?"

They said, "Her name is Bitisho."

"Okay," my dad replied.

"That is why we came here," they said.

"Okay—we accept you. Go and tell Mathias that we accept him in our family," my dad said.

After about two to three months, my future father-in-law came to our home again and asked for the dowry that included 15 cows. "If your son really wants to marry my daughter, you need to bring 20 cows," my family's spokesperson said.

Normally, it only requires 4 cows to marry, but my dad was still upset and wanted to make Mathias run away. Fortunately, Mathias's family had plenty of cows, 1,000 to be exact, so the 20 cows that my dad asked for were not going to put a strain on him or his family. My dad was shocked because, in his mind, he thought they would say no. They made an appointment to go and choose the cows from the farm one Sunday.

When they were shown the cows, Mathias' dad said, "If you don't see any you like, we have others in another section of the farm."

It was overwhelming, and when they came home, my mom said, "Oh my goodness, Mathias' dad has so many cows. We were surprised and confused, but we chose 15 cows. "

After settling the cow situation, we had to organize the next ceremony of bringing African clothing, shoes, earrings, and a watch. My Mom also received African clothing, a gift Mathias gave to my Mom for giving birth and taking care of my future wife. For me, I had my watch, clothing, and shoes – but no ring; however, now we were officially engaged.

Our wedding day was Saturday, May 27th, 1995. It was planned for two months and held in the Catholic Church. It was beautiful. My family and his family brought money for the food, and we had an area where we had the party after our wedding ceremony. Since my dad and father-in-law were wealthy, they would compete with each other over the gifts they gave us.

On the morning of our wedding, Mathias came to pick me up and gave me flowers. That meant that our marriage was official. If the groom does not bring the bride-to-be flowers, then it means the man doesn't want to marry the person. Giving flowers means he has accepted you. We went to the church, and I received my gold wedding ring during the ceremony. And I gave Mathias his gold wedding ring, which we still wear today. After the ceremony, we enjoyed a soiree in the building next to the church, given by our parents.

In our tradition, the cow that your husband gives for the dowry is sold, and things are bought for the kitchen, such as plates, pots, utensils, clothing, everything you can imagine. The husband provides furniture and the house, and then all the items are brought to that house. It felt good to both of us that they accepted us in the end. That was the happiest day of our lives.

In our tradition, a woman is not supposed to sleep with her husband-to-be before the wedding day. However, I did. The night of a wedding, they will send your grandma or aunt to be with you and sleep in another room. In the morning, she will ask for the sheets that should have blood on them. We didn't have that because we had been together before our wedding. When a grandma and aunt are brought to the family, they are supposed to be able to say, "Your daughter was a virgin on her wedding day, but that didn't happen. Fortunately, they didn't make a big deal of it, but in our tradition, we are supposed to wait until we get married. After the wedding, the bride is supposed to be with the mother-in-law so she can teach and welcome you into the family. In our case, I didn't stay with my mother-in-law, who lived in the village, even though my parents thought we would end up living in the village.

My sister divorced her husband, and unfortunately, her marriage was not good, and that was in the back of my dad's mind all the time. That is why he didn't want me to get married. He thought the same thing would happen to me, and he didn't want to see me suffer. One of the reasons my dad kept refusing to allow us to get married is because when I got my diploma, I received it with a 62% rating, a very high grade. The norm is 50%, and he said, "You are smart – you have to go to college. You can go to any college or university you want." The fact that my sister's marriage failed made it difficult for him to change his mind. I understood how he felt, but I was in love.

After our wedding, I stayed with Mathias, who was living in our town at the time. We planned to stay there for two weeks and then go to Burundi, where he was working as a teacher in a high school. He also found me a job in the library there, but by that time, the war was going on in Burundi (a neighboring country), and it wasn't safe.

We ended up staying with Mathias' sister for 8 months, and four months into our marriage, I found out I was pregnant. Her husband had four wives, so you can imagine they had quite a large family. While living there, I did the cooking and took care of the home, but four months into my pregnancy, it became too much for me to do all that work for that many people, especially while pregnant.

We decided to move and found our own apartment, and that is where my son, Harley, was born on June 15th, 1996. Then, in October of 1996, the First Congo War broke out as Rwanda increasingly expressed concern that Hutu members of Rassemblement Démocratique pour le Rwanda (RDR) militias were carrying out cross-border raids from what was then Zaire and planned an invasion of Rwanda which was located in Central/Eastern Africa and bordered by the Democratic Republic of the Congo to the west, Uganda to the north, Tanzania to the east, and Burundi to the south. It lies a few degrees south of the equator and is landlocked. The capital, Kigali, is located near the center of Rwanda.

The most deciding event in precipitating the war was the genocide in neighboring Rwanda in 1994, which sparked a mass exodus of refugees known as the Great Lakes refugee crisis. During the 100-day genocide, hundreds of thousands of Tutsis and sympathizers Hutus were massacred at the hands of predominantly Hutu aggressors. Ultimately, nine African countries and around twenty-five armed groups became involved in the war. By 2008, the war and its aftermath had caused 5.4 million deaths, principally through disease and starvation, making the Second Congo War the deadliest conflict worldwide since World War II. Now you understand why we had to flee.

THE WAR – HAD TO FLEE

The First Congo War, also nicknamed "Africa's First World War began in 1996 as Rwanda increasingly expressed concern that Hutu members of Rassemblement Democratique pour le Rwanda (RDR) militias were carrying out cross-border raids from what was then Zaire and planning an invasion of Rwanda. It was a civil war but also an international military conflict that took place mostly in Zaire (present-day Democratic Republic of Congo), with major spillovers into Sudan and Uganda.

The most deciding event in precipitating the war was the genocide in neighboring Rwanda in 1994, which sparked a mass exodus of refugees known as the Great Lakes refugee crisis. During the 100-day genocide, hundreds of thousands of Tutsis and sympathizers were massacred at the hands of predominantly Hutu aggressors. We had no choice but to flee our country.

When the war broke out in 1996, I was 24 years old, and we fled to Tanzania and stayed there for about one month. My whole family fled, and since my dad had bought a good-sized boat, instead of using it for business, we used it for the whole family. However, Mathias didn't go with us, hoping rebels would not take over our home city. However, it turned out that he was wrong. Eventually, Mathias joined us in Kigoma, Tanzania, and left after one month to go to Zambia. We stayed only one week and then took the bus to Zimbabwe. We stayed there for a short time before heading to Botswana to seek political asylum.

In Botswana, we had to make a statement as to why we ran from our country. Mathias explained that if we stayed, most likely, we would have been killed. Unfortunately, the Botswana government could not accept us because they only accept people from neighboring countries. Since we had gone through two other countries to get there, they would not accept us and turned us over to the United Nations High Commission for Refugees (UNHCR) to help us find another country where we could go to live. They took us to Dukwi Refugee Camp, where we lived for three and a half years before making our way to the United States.

We arrived in Gaborone, the capital city of Botswana, on a certain Friday evening and didn't know anybody. We had to look for the UNHCR office and asked a taxi driver if he knew anything about the United Nations.

He said, "I don't know. I believe they are located in a tall building downtown." Since it was already late, Mathias asked him if he could drop us off at the nearby and cheapest motel.

"Sure," he replied, taking us to the motel where we stayed for the weekend. On Saturday morning, Mathias went downtown and found the United Nations office, but the office was closed since it was a weekend. No one was working on Saturday.

First thing Monday morning, we all went to the office with our son, who was 7 months old, and our niece, my husband's sister's daughter. She was staying with us at the time that we fled, so we had to take her with us. She never went back to her Mom. At first, it was fine as we didn't think much about it and just wanted her to be safe. However, when we arrived in Botswana, we started thinking about having this child who is not ours.

We didn't know the situation back home, so I asked Mathias, "What are we going to do?"

"We have to keep her," he said.

"No – we have to bring her back home," I replied.

"How?" he asked.

I had no answers, so we ended up bringing her with us.

Mathias told me to wait in the parking lot while he went into the UN High Commission Refugees office. I was carrying my baby on my back and holding my niece's hand when I looked over and saw the police in the parking lot. It turned out that they were security guards, but I kept thinking they were the police. Keep in mind that I didn't speak English at this point, and I was with my baby and didn't belong in Botswana. My heart was pounding out of my chest because we didn't have any legal papers to stay in Botswana, and our visa had expired. The security guards kept looking at me, and I knew it was our end. Mathias still had not come back and I didn't know what to do.

After about 30 minutes, he came walking back toward us and said, "You know what? They are going to help us, and they told me to come and get you and the kids."

We walked into this enormous building and took the elevator up to the sixth floor. Once in the office with the woman from the UN High Commission for Refugees, the protection officer's secretary started asking us all sorts of questions. "What happened?" she asked. Mathias provided all the details about the reasons or circumstances in which we left our home country, and we had no choice but to flee for our lives. "We feared being killed or imprisoned because we did not have the same political opinions," Mathias added.

"Oh my gosh," the woman replied. She said: "We have to ask the Botswana government if they can accept to grant you political asylum; however, we are not sure if they will because you were supposed to stay in one of the neighboring countries with the Democratic Republic of Congo: Angola, Zimbabwe, Central Africa Republic, Sudan, Uganda, Congo-Brazzaville, Zambia, Rwanda, or Tanzania."

She turned and called the Special Branch (intelligence agency service) agents, who showed up and took us to their office next to the police station. They started asking us more questions again about why we had crossed into the country. They put me in one room and my husband in another room, but they only spoke English. We were taught English in school but didn't know the language well enough to converse with them.

One of the agents asked me, "You don't have anyone in Botswana? Any family? How did you get here?"

"We just ran to save our lives," I repeated many times. I knew that we would be okay as refugees without papers or a visa.

"How did you find yourself in Botswana?" the special branch agent asked again. They wanted to know if there was some organization that was bringing people over the border.

When the war started, we had a priest who helped us get out of there. He hired a truck driver, and we rode in the back of his truck as we crossed through all three countries. When we arrived in Botswana, the driver said, "You are safe here. Go and look for someone who can help you."

When we got out of the truck, we had no idea where we were, but we found ourselves in Botswana.

The Special Branch agent looked at me and asked, "You have a baby? The baby didn't die in the back of the truck?"

"No," I replied.

"How did you go to the bathroom?" the agent asked.

"We had plastic bags to do our business," I replied.

It was around 6 pm in the evening, and they kept asking if we knew anyone.

"Now that it is the end of the workday, where are you going to go?" the agent asked me.

"We don't know," I answered. Just then, the door opened, and they brought milk for the baby and fast food for us.

"We are not finished here; you will need to come back tomorrow morning – Tuesday – to finish this interrogation," the agent explained. "We want to know what really happened."

"Okay—but we don't know where to go," Mathias said as we were together again.

The officer who was asking all the questions went to the police chief and asked, "Can you give them somewhere to stay?"

We ended up staying in the hallways of the jail. The next morning, they came back to find us and started questioning us again. "Who is this baby?" the agent asked.

"He is ours," I replied.

"Who is this other child?" he asked.

"She is our niece," Mathias stated.

"How come you are here with her?" he asked.

"She came to our place for the summer break, and when the war broke out, we couldn't just leave her. That is why we have her," my husband explained.

"That is okay," the UNHCR attendant said as she walked in and sat down. "You will have to make a separate file for your niece."

"Okay," she went on to say, "We will send you to the Botswana Council for Refugees (BCR). Finally, at the end of all that questioning, around 5:00 PM, the UNHCR officer called them and said, "We have a family we are bringing to you." When we arrived there, we met with the BCR director, who asked us what had happened again. It was exhausting.

"Since you are with us, we will be taking care of you," the director said. We were actually in the capital of Botswana. We were happy with that because they saw we had the baby and our niece. They gave us diapers, milk for the baby, food, and they had one room for us where we slept.

The director said to us, "The Dukwi refugee camp is about 200-300 miles away. We have we have field officers who take refugees there. Tomorrow morning, you will catch the train and go to the refugee camp."

That is what we did; fortunately, they gave us food for traveling on the train. We traveled to Francistown, and they sent a camp driver to pick us up at the train station. As soon as we arrived at the camp, they gave us food, clothing, pots, plates and pans, a small stove to cook our food, a lamp, kerosene to light the lamp, a stove, and mattresses. Since we were a family, we were given a small house with two rooms, and in the middle, there was a veranda. If one is single, they are given one room, so we are grateful to have a house for our family.

We received food every 15 days, basically two times a month, according to the number of family members. That equated to 12.5 kilos of cornmeal for each person in our family, so we received 50 kilos of cornmeal, 4 kilos of beans, 4 kilos of rice, 5 liters of cooking oil, and kerosene to light the lamp and the stove. Since I had the baby, we were also given milk and diapers.

After we were settled, the UN High Commission for Refugees transferred our file to the Botswana government representative who manages the Dukwi refugee camp. Based on what we had told them upon our arrival, the Botswana laws would not allow us to settle in their country as refugees. One has to be from a neighboring country, as I mentioned earlier, in order to get asylum, but we did not meet their criteria. They had to look for a third country that would take us as we couldn't return to our home country, the Democratic Republic of Congo.

In the refugee camp, they had projects that were mainly for women; however, when I went to the meeting, I couldn't understand what they were saying. Fortunately, I found another woman who could explain it all to me and I discovered they had all sorts of projects that included working on the farm.

One of the attendants asked me, "Which one do you want?"

"Maybe chickens?" I replied.

They gave me fifty chicks that had hatched that day, and then they gave me fifty more chickens that lay eggs only. At this point, we had only been in the refugee camp for two weeks. Food for the chicks and the chickens was also given to us, and that allowed us to raise and sell the eggs and the chickens. During those three and half years, we took care of chickens, but I also made donuts with the money we made from selling the chickens and eggs. We had a guy who would bring us firewood for cooking, and in return, we gave him some of our food.

After one month in the refugee camp, I was pregnant, and fortunately, a small clinic offered pre-natal care in the camp. Living out in a desert where the camp was located and caring for all those chickens while pregnant was not easy, even though I was twenty-three years old. My son was eight months old, and I was pregnant with another baby.

Mathias offered to help me and would wake up every morning to take care of the chickens, clean the pens, and feed them at the poultry. After eight weeks, they would be sold, but it was quite the adjustment.

Nine months later, in the early morning hours of November 10th, 1997, I knew the baby was coming, but I couldn't walk anymore. Mathias ran to get the wheelbarrow he had kept behind the house, carefully put me in it, and wheeled me to the clinic. Unfortunately, the clinic was closed, but the cleaning crew was still there. Immediately, they called one of the nurses who came right away. Within two hours, I gave birth at 7:30 in the morning to my baby, Melissa who was almost 9 pounds. Around three in the afternoon, I was sent home and managed to walk across the street – no wheelbarrow rides this time because Mathias was at the poultry to feed the chickens. The nurses would check on me and the baby every morning.

After about three years of living in the refugee camp, we were finally accepted by the United States of America government, and the process of immigration began with a background check. Then, we had a physical check-up to ensure we were healthy enough to make the trip. We asked for our marriage certificate but lost it when we fled the country. We showed them our picture from our wedding day, but we needed more and would suffice the legal paper requirement. As a result, we had to get married for the second time on July 8th, 1999.

We held the civil wedding in Francistown, the second-largest city in Botswana. Since we did not have any family members with us, we had to have two persons to help us out as witnesses. So, close refugee friends Paul and Jose agreed to be our civil wedding witnesses. After the wedding ceremonies, we had dinner at the local restaurant before returning to Dukwi refugee camp. Our children and niece were also with us at our civil wedding ceremonies.

For the next six months, the UNHCR worked on our travel papers to go through immigration. Upon arriving in the United States, we also had the opportunity to watch a documentary about the American culture and life of refugees. Finally, on August 8, 2000, we traveled from Botswana via Johannesburg (South Africa), Brussels (Belgium), and New York before arriving in San Francisco, California, on August 9th, 2000.

WHY CALIFORNIA?

4

W hen we were informed by the United Nations High Commission for Refugees that the United States government accepted us, we were not told where we were going initially. Eventually, we were told we would be landing in San Francisco, though we didn't know why that particular city was chosen. Traveling from Botswana to California took us 18 hours, not including waiting time. All I remember is that my feet were so swollen from sitting for so many hours when we arrived. All we had with us was our clothing and $100 from the sale of our chickens. We had given some of the money to some friends before leaving Botswana so they could keep taking care of the chickens for themselves.

When we arrived at the airport in San Francisco at around six in the evening, we walked into the baggage claim area and saw so many people standing around waiting for relatives and other passengers. We kept looking for the person we were told was going to pick us up and finally found a man holding a sign with my husband's last name, "Mulengwa." Mathias said to me, "He must be the one who will guide us."

We approached him, introduced ourselves, and said, "We are the Mulengwa family."

"Wonderful," he said as he explained that he was a case worker working for the International Rescue Committee (IRC).

The IRC is a non-profit, federally funded government organization helping refugees settle in the U.S. The name of the gentleman who was waiting for us at the San Francisco International Airport was Tom, and before we arrived, he knew that we were a family of five and that we spoke French. Tom was with a young woman who volunteered with the IRC and spoke French, so we felt very lucky that we had these two people meet us at the airport. As we started walking to their vehicle, I asked Mathias, "How did they know we speak French? We didn't have any communication with them."

Fortunately, she was helping us translate from French to English so that Tom could communicate with us. Once we were in the car, he said to us, "I know you are supposed to live in San Francisco, but the cost of living is so high in that city. As a refugee, it would be quite difficult for you to start out there, so I will be bringing you to Oakland. It is right next to San Francisco, and the cost of living is much cheaper."

It was around 8 pm at night when we crossed the San Francisco bridge, and all we could say was, "Wow! Look at all those beautiful lights." The whole city seemed to glow, and it was the first time we had seen something like that. After crossing the bridge, Tom brought us to a hotel in Oakland. Once we were in the hotel, through the interpreter, he said, "You should stay here in the hotel, and I will look for an apartment for you. Once we find one, I will pick you up and take you there."

We ended up staying in that hotel for two weeks. Every day, he would bring us food and update us on his progress in finding housing with the interpreter. The time change was a bit difficult to adjust to because at night, it would be daytime in Africa, and vice versa so we slept during the day and would wake up around 8 pm. It took a little while for our systems to adjust to the time change.

After two weeks of eating fast food and a lot of bread for breakfast, lunch, and dinner, I couldn't wait until we could move to an apartment so I could cook a meal. Finally, it was time to move, and Tom paid our hotel bill, picked us up, and moved us to a two-bedroom apartment. He was always with the interpreter, and they gave us everything we needed: mattresses, pots, pans, dishes, a table with four chairs, five plates, four knives, and four forks, but I said to him, "There are five in our family, our niece, Harley, Melissa, and us." I started feeling weird about the whole situation immediately, but we made it work. At the time, our children were very young – Harley was over 3 years old, Melissa was over two years old, and our niece, Cheka, was ten years old at the time.

After we put all of our supplies inside the apartment, he took us to the local grocery store so we could buy food. It made me happy to see food from home, but the first thing I noticed was how big the store was – it was huge. I remarked that there was no smell of the fruit in the produce section. I said to Mathias, "If you leave a banana in the house and close the door when you come home, you can smell it."

There were so many fruits and vegetables in that grocery store, but when I went to smell the pineapple, I expected it to have a strong smell. After all, we lived in a tropical area for a long time, but it didn't have any aroma. Everyone in the store looked nice, and everything we wanted was there. We bought what we needed for the week, including milk, bread, and a huge chicken; even the onions were big. We had been eating so much bread for the past couple of weeks I was eager to cook the chicken.

"Do they have flour here?" I asked, looking at Mathias.

"I don't know – let's ask the people in the store," he replied.

We bought some corn flour, went home, and cooked the chicken in boiling water with tomatoes and onions. It felt so good to eat fresh food again. It tasted great, but I realized that the chicken is different from the chicken back home. It was so big that it took forever to cook and ended up being a bit tough and a bit of a disappointment. I used the corn flour meal and made a fu-fu dough, then cooked vegetables, including collard greens, and those tasted okay.

Most of the time, we drink water, but I will never forget the first time I saw all the 2-liter bottles of Coca-Cola in the grocery store and said to Mathias, "Oh my goodness – these are so big." We were used to drinking small servings of Coca-Cola in a thin glass bottle but looked at soft drinks as a special treat.

After a few days, Tom from IRC came to our apartment with the interpreter and told us we needed to bring the kids to the Children's Hospital so we could get a check-up for the whole family. The kids had to get immunizations because it would be time for them to start pre-school. He also showed us what we needed to know as far as getting the bus, other local stores, and what we needed to know for daily life.

When we moved into the apartment, an African American neighbor stopped by to say hello and introduced himself. Since we didn't know much English, it wasn't easy to communicate with each other, but he was very kind, and it felt good to meet someone close by. He showed us where the preschool was located, and when we met with the principal to enroll our kids, we had to show proof of income. Since we didn't have any income at that time, it was easy for the kids to be admitted, as the preschool was for low-income families. The preschool center had four rooms for each age group of three-, four-, and five- and six-year-old children. Since Melissa was only two years and nine months at the time, they could not accept her because she was not quite three years old.

"Does she use diapers?" he asked.

"No," I replied.

"If she doesn't use diapers, then she can come, but we need permission from her doctor," he said. "By law, she has to be three years old."

"Okay," I replied, and she was accepted at two years and nine months of age.

He said, "However, there is one condition - in order for your kids to be accepted, you and Mathias have to be going to school or working – you have to be doing something for us to accept your children."

"We can do that," we said in unison.

The next day, Tom came by, and we told him the situation: "They will accept our children, but we have to do something, go to school or work."

"Okay," he said. "In the IRC program, we can help refugees for three months, pay your rent and you will receive $200 a month for food."

Our niece, Cheka, went to the elementary school across the street from where we lived, starting in fifth grade.

When the kids were enrolled in school, we had a chance to look for a job. Tom put the word out that we were looking for work, and our landlord was also keeping an eye out for a work opportunity. By the time November rolled around, it had been three months, so I decided to go to school to become a certified nursing assistant. The program lasted 3 to 6 months, and since nursing assistants were in high demand, I knew it would provide a way to make a living. Actually, when you enroll in the school, you are paid a minimum wage for every hour you are in the classroom.

At the end of the program, I started working as a nursing assistant at the Oakland Rehabilitation Center. Both my husband and I wanted to do the program because after you get certified, they can hire you right away. In the year 2000, I was getting a minimum wage of $7 per hour while our kids were going to preschool. Once I started working, I wouldn't say I liked it, though I was grateful for a job. It was so depressing seeing all these old people living under one roof. In Africa, they don't have nursing homes. My parents took care of my grandparents, and we are expected to take care of our parents, and so on. Even though I didn't like my job, I said to Mathias, "We are here now, and we have to take care of our family. We are doing what we need to do."

Our schedules couldn't be more different because I worked from 7 a.m. to 3 p.m. in the morning, and Mathias worked from 3 p.m. until 11 p.m., so someone would be home when the kids got out of preschool. It was a difficult time because we hardly saw each other, and we were still learning English. In Africa, they teach English, but it is English from England, not America.

The first time someone said to me, "Hi."

I didn't know how to answer because, in England, you would say, "Good Morning" or "Good Evening."

"What is Hi?" I asked.

"It's a greeting," the person replied, looking at me like I was from outer space. "You can say 'Hi' back."

"Okay," I replied. "You don't say good morning?"

"Yes – you can say good morning – but 'Hi" is what we say here," she said. When it came to our kids, we didn't teach them much Swahili because they needed to learn English.

Mathias and I went to school for our training in two different facilities. Since we didn't have a car, I had to walk to work for one year before finding out there was another facility closer to our apartment. I worked there for three years, and when I came home after picking up the kids, Mathias would leave and go to work. They were at school from 7 am until 5 pm, so it was a long day for them. By the time we had dinner, it was time to go to bed. That was our schedule for each day. Grocery shopping was even more difficult since we didn't have a car.

In 2001, we were finally able to buy our first car, a brand new; it was Daewoo Nubira, a South Korean car. At first, Mathias looked in the Yellow Pages to find a driving school so he could get his driver's license and learn how to drive. Once he got his driver's license, we bought the car. I still didn't know how to drive, and though Mathias offered to teach me, every time we would get in the car to practice driving, we would end up not talking to each other the rest of the day – LOL.

I said to him, "Don't teach me anymore – let me hire the teacher back to teach me because this isn't working."

One time, I went to work and came home to discover Mathias had bought a car – he was so happy.

"You bought a car?" I said in surprise. "How much did you pay?"

"Well – we had $10,000 in our savings, and I used all that to buy the car," he said.

I was upset and said, "Now we have zero money in savings."

"We don't have any credit history," Mathias explained. "No one knows us here, and we need to establish credit, so I decided to give them $10,000 for a down payment. The total cost of the car is $21,000."

When Tom from the IRC came back, he took us to the bank so we could open our first joint checking account. He told us, "In

America, you have to have a credit history to buy a car, house, or even a washer and dryer. This will help you build up your credit history."

After we opened that account at the bank, we went back after one month and tried to open a credit card account. The banker asked us, "How long have you been here?"

"We are new here to this country," we replied.

Even though we had all the legal papers to live in the U.S., including our social security numbers, work permit and IDs, the bank denied us the credit card account because we needed to have established credit. That is why Mathias purchased the car, so we could establish credit. Our car payment per month was less than $200, and while we still had to pay back what it cost to bring us here to the U.S. from Africa so they could help others, establishing our credit history would allow us to do more things, including buying a house.

Since we had paid $10,000 for the car, our rent was only $750 per month, and we were paid every two weeks, so we would use one check to pay rent and other bills, another two-week check to pay for groceries, and the other two-week paychecks would go in our savings account. As a result, we were able to save $10,000 in less than a year, ten months actually, and paid for our first car. By doing that, it helped establish our credit from the car that we had purchased. Since we paid a large amount as a down payment, our monthly payment was less than $200 per month. It just goes to show that when you take the time to make a financial plan, it allows you to do more things in your life, buy a house, and still live comfortably. We were grateful to be in the U.S. without dealing with a war that seemed never to end.

Bitisho after graduating high school
1994

Bitisho and Mathias on a windy day on the beach

Mathias and Bitisho at the beach Uvira, Democratic Republic of Conga
One year before our wedding July of 1994

Bitisho in my Mom's bedroom waiting for Mathias to come and bring
flowers to give to me before going to church for our wedding.
May 27, 1995

Mathias and Bitisho wedding day about to shake hands with my Dad
Catholic Cathedral in Uvira
May 27, 1995

Our wedding day in Uvira Catholic Church
Saturday May 27, 1995

Bitisho's Dad saying a toast on our wedding day

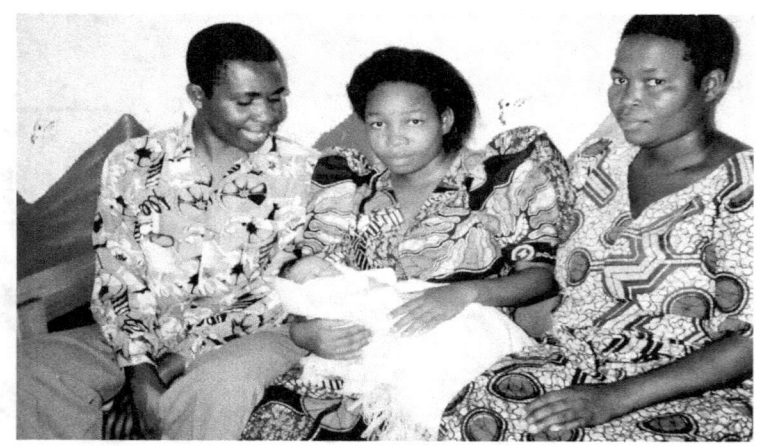

Mathias, Bitisho, Harley, and my sister,
Charlotte Two days after Harley was born June 17, 1996

Bitisho 8 months pregnant with Melissa and Harley standing by in
Dukwi Refugee Camp In Botswana October 1997

Ten minutes after giving birth to Melissa Dukwi, Botswana
November 10, 1997

Cheka and Harley in Dukwi, Botswana Refugee Camp December 1998

Harley and Melissa posing August 1998

Harley, Bitisho, and Melissa before our second wedding ceremony
Francistown, Botswana July 8, 1999

Our second wedding day in Francistown, Botswana
July 8, 1999

Our last week in Sebena, Botswana in front of the Catholic Church
From left to right front row: Cheka, Harley, and Melissa
Back row: Mathias and Bitisho
August 6, 2000

Melissa, Bitisho, and Harley –
Our first picture taken after arriving in Oakland, California
August 2000

Going to Farmer's Market on
Sunday in Jack London Square in Oakland, California
October 2000

Bitisho's parents: Uzia and Rashidi in Kigoma, Tanzania at my brother, Alexis' wedding

At the Gaborone International Airport, the day we left Boswana
August 8, 2000

Harley (4) and Melissa (3) in our first apartment in
Oakland, California

Melissa and Harley throwing pennies in the fountain at Jack London's
Square in Oakland, California

Cheka, Melissa, Bitisho and Harley
First Christmas in the United States December 2000

Our first Christmas in the United States December 2000

Graduation Day for Associates Degree from Heald College July 2003

Volunteering for a United Nations International
Emergency Fund (UNICEF) in Berkley, California
2003

Bitisho's Mom, Uzia
2003 in Uvira, Democratic Republic of Congo

The day of our U.S. citizenship
December 15, 2005

Bitisho's brother, Alexis and Bitisho when he came to visit us from Montreal, Canada after not seeing each other for ten years.
Summer of 2007

Bitisho's 40 birthday in our first house in Salinas, California
June 1, 2010

At the Monterey Aquarium –
Bitisho's Mom and Dad when they came to visit
December 27, 2011

Our first Christmas
December 2000

Mathias and Bitisho in our first apartment in Oakland,
California 2002

Bitisho's Dad, Harley and Bitisho at Excellence Award Ceremony
Harden Middle School in Salinas, California
December 2011

Dad, Mom and Bitisho when they came to visit us in Salinas, California
December 2011

Bitisho and Mom, Uzia in Salinas, California
December of 2011

Melissa's graduation picture from San Francisco State University Master's Degree in Business Administration June 2020

Bitisho and Mathias in Salinas before going out dinner

Bitisho, Harley and Mathias at graduation getting his
Bachelor's degree from Chico State

Melissa getting her Bachelor's Degree in Public Health from UC Irvine

Melissa and Harley on Christmas Day 2016

Melissa's graduation day where we came to show our support

Harley
and

Melissa
In Downtown Salinas

Bitisho and Melissa on the way to a friend's wedding

Harley and Mathias before going to a friend's wedding

Big Sur Visit

Harley graduation with his Master's Degree in
Business Administration

At home celebrating our 24th wedding anniversary

Melissa at UC Irvine party

At home in our living room before our date night

Celebrating Christmas Day 2019

At UC Irvine visiting Melissa

LIFE IN OAKLAND

L ife in Oakland was good; by then, 75% of the community was Black. When we arrived, it felt like I was home and didn't feel like an outsider. Oakland is very similar to the climate in my hometown living near a lake with the ocean nearby and its warm breeze. Summer is nice here, and we don't ever get snow. I only want to watch it on TV. A place nearby makes fake snow during the winter months, which is fun to experience, but that is the only time I have seen snow.

Even though I got certified as a nursing assistant to get paid more for working at the nursing home, I soon realized that nursing was not for me. I was doing the work to survive as a Mom and make a living, though I did learn a lot about caring for the elderly and end-of-life care. It taught me to enjoy every second of my life because I can see how that can end. That old saying, "If you are doing what you love – you never work a day in your life," is so true.

After two years of working as a nursing assistant, I decided to go back to school and went to Heald College in Hayward, California, not too far from Oakland. However, I was not driving on the freeway at that time because of my previous car accident.

Even though I knew how to drive, I was scared of driving and could drive myself from home to work every day.

"How are you going to go to that school without driving on the freeway?" Mathias asked me one day.

"We have a bus and subway system," I replied, thinking that was my best option.

Mathias said to me, "I will go to school with you."

"Really?" I said in surprise. That was nice of him because he already had his bachelor's degree.

He said, "I need to go with you so I can learn English from college."

We made that decision together so in the morning, we took the kids to the daycare center and went to school from 8 am until 2 pm in the afternoon. I told my employer at the nursing home center that I would be going to school during the week and could work on the weekends only. That is exactly what I did for two years. I went to school Monday through Friday and worked at the nursing center on the weekends. Mathias was working, too, so as soon as we would get home from school, he would shower, change clothes, and go to work, and he did that for two years.

In July of 2003, I am proud to say that I received my Associate Applied (AA) degree in computer business software application. However, during the middle of the school year, Mathias changed his major and had to take one more semester of classes, so as a result, I graduated before him. One month before graduation, we decided to move to Monterey, California, because Mathias found a school, the Monterey Institute of International Studies, where he could get his master's degree. Besides being a one-hour drive, the cost of living was quite high in Monterey, so we decided to move to Salinas, which reduced it to a 25-minute drive.

Even though we had the idea to move, and I had my degree, I didn't want to leave my nursing job, so I went back to tell my employer that I wanted my full-time job back.

"Do you want to come back again as a nurse's assistant?" she asked, surprised.

"Yes," I replied.

We needed more money so we could make our move, but instead of moving to an apartment, we wanted a house. In order to save money, I had to work more overtime, which means 16 - 18 hours a day. It was so hard, especially when Mathias was off work. I worked from 7 am to 11 pm every day. We were both working so hard and long hours that we rarely saw each other. In fact, I remember Mathias asking me if I could cut his hair one night because it had grown so much. We were like ships passing in the night, but we kept those crazy schedules to save up enough money to make a down payment on a house.

After extensive research online, I discovered a brand-new housing development in Salinas where they built new homes. We had paid off our car in four years, one year earlier than our loan required, so that gave us more money towards a house. When I called the new development, they told me I needed to find a realtor, and when I found the realtor, she said to us, "You can make this happen with $30,000." Knowing that was how much money we needed gave us more encouragement to work even harder. Any time we could get overtime hours, we took it because we were paid time and a half for those extra hours.

We finally saved $30,000 for the down payment, and our realtor negotiated the house deal for us in 2004. Even though the housing development had their preferred lender, we ended up going elsewhere for the loan and chose a 1600-square foot home with 3 bedrooms, 2 ½ baths, and a 2-car garage. The price of the house was $350,000, and the housing market went up every month. It took six months to build our house after we chose the lot and block we wanted and signed the contract the same day.

This gave us six more months to work and save more money, but every month, the price of our home went up by $10,000, and by the time we moved in, our home was worth $400,000. We did zero down, which made our house payment higher, and by the time we paid taxes, which are quite high in California, we realized this was an expensive proposition, but we knew nothing about buying a house, and we were still learning how to live in America.

The $30,000 we saved paid for the closing costs, taxes, and new furniture, but we were excited to start a new life. We moved into our new home in October of 2004. Isn't it amazing? We arrived in California in August of 2000, and four years later, we bought a brand-new home. We both had good jobs and degrees, our kids were doing well in school, and life was good.

In Salinas, 80% of the population is Latino, so it was quite a new environment for us after living in Oakland, where we felt a part of the Black community. When we went to the bank to ask for a credit card, they said, "No," because we had never had a credit card before. We always paid cash for everything we needed. If we needed something, we would work hard to save enough money to pay for it. Even though buying the car helped establish our credit, we decided that the only credit we would ever apply for was our mortgage, car loan, or student loans for our education.

After we closed on our house, we had $3,000 left, so we put a down payment on a second car so we could work at different places if needed. We found a brand-new Kia Sedona Mini Van that I drove. After a year of living in our new home, the value of it was still going up, so we refinanced it. We took $50,000 from the equity in our home and paid off the KIA Sedona, which was $20,000, took $20,000 and bought the property back home where we were born so my mother-in-law could live in that house, which she loved, and the other $10,000 went into our savings account.

When we moved to Salinas in October 2004, it was easier for me to continue working as a certified nursing assistant, but I was looking for another job in my field. I finally found a job at the First National Bank of Central California as a customer service representative like a teller. They didn't give me full-time work right away and only worked part-time, but after six months, they gave me a full-time position. Since I wouldn't say I liked wearing the uniform as a certified nursing assistant, I really enjoyed my new position at the bank because now I had to wear nice clothes with jewelry and make-up. And I loved meeting new people every day.

We continued to build equity in our home, and after two years of living there, we bought our second home in Salinas in another neighborhood. We found another area where they were building new homes again, but by that time, we had so much equity in our first home that we bought a much larger second home, 2700 square feet with 5 bedrooms, 3 bathrooms, and a spacious 2-car garage. It was a very nice home.

Meanwhile, we found a tenant to rent our first house and hired a property manager to manage that property while we lived in our second home. The money that we made from that house helped pay for our mortgage. Mathias went back to Monterey Institute of International Studies (MIIS) to get his master's degree in international business so he would drive from Salinas to Monterey every day to go to school. We were doing quite well and enjoying our big, new house.

However, in 2007, the housing market started going down, which meant the value of both our homes was going down. Our second home cost $680,000 and was located in a beautiful neighborhood, but when the housing market started to collapse, people simply left the area, letting their homes go into foreclosure. Instead of the value going up, we were paying more on the mortgage, so we decided we were going to have to leave our second house and move back to our first house.

The property manager told the tenant he had to move out so we could move back in and stopped paying our mortgage. We had only lived there for three months before we had to foreclose on it. We found a bankruptcy lawyer who explained what was happening and made recommendations for what we should do. Following his advice, we paid our fee and were told to appear in court for legal proceedings. Fortunately, the bank did not show up for our court date at the courthouse, and the judge ruled in our favor, which meant we didn't have to pay anything. By that time, the banks didn't know who was doing what, which made it confusing for everyone. Before that time, we had tried to negotiate a lower monthly payment with the bank, but they refused, so we had to let go of the home and file bankruptcy.

After our lawyer did all the paperwork at the courthouse, we were thrilled that we didn't have to pay anything. He said to us, "You need to go home, relax, and start over. This is not a crime. If anyone calls you asking for the money, give them my number."

We moved out of our first house and rented an apartment, starting life all over again. We started saving money again to clear our credit history since it was so bad from filing for bankruptcy. We bought another car from the same place we had purchased one before, and from that car, we started making monthly payments again, and after seven years, we finished paying off the car and created a good credit history.

Eventually, we bought another new home in a different neighborhood in Salinas that took six months to build, saving our money and going through that process all over again. In the meantime, our kids were growing fast, and our niece had graduated from Sacramento State University with a bachelor's degree in education. Though it was difficult at times for our kids to move from a predominantly Black community to Salinas, which was 80% Latino, they both did well in school.

THE KIDS

You may recall our niece, Cheka, who we took with us when we fled our country. It turns out her Mom passed away in 2014, so she never saw her Mom again. While we didn't adopt her, we became her legal guardian. In our culture, we don't adopt children like the adoption process is done here in the U.S. It is different back home because any child from our siblings or family can have the name and live with them without any legal papers. If a child needs a home, you help that child where you can.

Every child belongs to God and every child has their own clan. My clan is different from my husband's. We belong to our clan, so I can't just put you in my clan. She came to live with us when she was six years old. She is doing so well today, has a bachelor's degree in education, is married, and has two children. We couldn't be prouder of her and her accomplishments.

Since we arrived in the United States when our children were so young, it was easy for them to adapt because Harley was three and Melissa was two. We were grateful for the child development center that opened at 7 a.m., where they would have breakfast before school started, and then after school, they were there until 5 p.m. The Henriette Tubman Daycare Center was helping them with their homework, which was really helpful for us since we were both so busy working and learning English, too. As refugees and parents without childcare or much money when we arrived in the U.S., the daycare center was a Godsend.

They went to Hoover Elementary School in Oakland when they were old enough to start school at six years old. We moved from Oakland to Salinas when Melissa was eight years old going into 3rd grade and Harley was nine years old starting 4th grade at Salinas Steinbeck Elementary school, named after the famous Salinas author.

Going from a predominantly Black community to a Latino community where Harley and Melissa were now in the minority was quite a shock for them, as they didn't understand and asked, "Where are all the Black people?" From the first day of school, when they came home, you should have seen the look on their faces when Harley told me, "I was the only Black person in the classroom."

I told him, "Honey, we are in Salinas now, and most of the people who live here are Latino, but as human beings, we are all different shades of color."

One incident that took place in the classroom with Melissa's teacher involved her system of cards that were red, yellow, or green, with green meaning a student was a good student. If anyone did something bad or wrong, they would receive a different-colored card. Melissa was a good student and always had a green card. At the end of the week, if the student had a green card, the other students would have to say something good about that student.

One student, who was asked to write something about Melissa, said, "I can't write anything good about her because she is Black."

When Melissa came home, she was so disappointed and felt sad. Immediately, I called the teacher to make an appointment for a meeting, and the teacher said, "I will take care of this."

I was told that she called the student's parents and said, "This is unacceptable behavior."

The next day, after school, when she came home, I said to Melissa, "You are Black, and we are all different shades. Your color does not mean you are a bad person. You are 'you,' a good, smart, and beautiful person. You need to respect everyone."

When it comes to our kids, we keep boosting their morale and self-esteem. Every night, we make sure we have dinner together to discuss any issues that occur during the day. We always tell them, "The color of your skin does not mean you can't do whatever you want to do with your life. Do you see anyone with three eyes or two noses? No. We are all the same. Focus on your studies, do your homework, and be respectful of other people."

We always discussed this at our dinner table at home. When either of them had a problem, we would always discuss it. With all the pressures of life, we had to prepare them for what they would face so they would be confident in life.

Another incident happened again in high school with Melissa involving the cover page for their school magazine. She was chosen to be on the cover and took a great picture. A girl came up to her and said, "You are very beautiful, and you could do modeling, but because you are Black, it probably won't help you."

I told her, "Don't believe that – God made us all different colors."

"Okay," she replied.

"When we moved from the hotel to our first apartment, the IRC agency came with photographers who were taking pictures of us to promote refugees for fundraising. Remember that?"

"Yes," she replied. "I remember that picture."

Melissa's picture was chosen for the postcard cover to raise fundraising money.

When she was born in Botswana, they gave her the name "Naledi," which means "Star," and thought that should be her name.

Mathias said, "No – I am not going to give that name to her. They didn't give us papers to live in Botswana, so we are not going to call her that." Looking back, I realize that the name Naledi has a special meaning.

When we told Melissa that story, she said, "I think that is a good name, and I can give that to my children one day."

All her life, she focused on her studies as we protected them. When they finished elementary school, they went to Harden Middle School before attending North Salinas High School. Once they graduated high school, Harley went to Chico State in Northern California to get his bachelor's degree in healthcare administration. The following year, Melissa went to the University of California (UC) in Irvine, California, to get her bachelor's degree in public health policy.

After Harley graduated from Chico, he went to Los Angeles State University to get his master's degree MBA and graduated in December of 2021. When the COVID-19 pandemic hit, he was in Los Angeles then, so he returned home and finished his program online.

Melissa graduated one semester before Harley in June of 2020 because while in high school, she took all the advanced classes for math and English at a community college during high school, so when she went to UC, she had credit for one year. Instead of going to college for four years, she graduated in 3 years with her bachelor's degree in public health policy at 20 years old.

At the age of twenty-two, she got her master's degree in business administration (MBA) from San Francisco State University.

Today, Melissa works in the budget department for the office of the president at University of California. It is quite an honor for her to serve as one of the budget analysts. Harley is still looking and applying for a variety of jobs, while Melissa is still working remotely from home due to the COVID-19 pandemic.

"I have to go back to my roots in Oakland, Mom," Melissa said. She always tells me that she is the youngest person in the room every time they have a meeting at work. Most people she works with are in their 30s and 40s, but we are so proud of her. We were surprised when she negotiated her pay and received a higher salary.

One day, she said to us, "I have an interview tomorrow."

"Really? Where?" I asked.

When she told us, she said, "I think I will get the job." After three days, she received notice that she had a second interview. After a week, they called her and offered her the job.

When she told us her salary, she said, "I can negotiate for more."

"Why do you want to negotiate? They are offering you a good salary per year. That is quite high, and they are giving you more than you were expecting, and you still want to negotiate?" I asked her.

She said, "As women, we don't negotiate enough and often take the first offer. Men usually get paid more after they start complaining."

"Melissa – take the job," I said with my heart pounding. "It is enough for you. After all, you are only 22, and starting that high is really good."

"I have to try," she insisted. "If I don't, I will regret it and could maybe get more."

"Are you going to be okay if they don't call you?" I asked.

"Yes – because I just want to try – if they don't give me more, that is fine," she replied emphatically. "I want to make history and believe I deserve it."

"You don't have experience," I argued. "You just graduated."

"I can reach six figures," she said with confidence.

"Even if they give you more, don't argue with them. Just take it," I said.

When it was time to negotiate, they gave her more than the original base salary and proved us wrong.

"We are very proud of you," I said. "You went to school, graduated, are doing well, and now we would like grandkids. How are we going to get grandkids if you are not dating? You have done what we expected of you. For the next stage in your life, you should start dating."

Since Melissa got her MBA, she has always wanted to open her own business. After graduating during the Covid-19 pandemic in June of 2020, she started building her online business called mommandmimba.com. 'Mimba' means pregnancy where items are sold online for pregnant women, particularly maternity dresses. She built everything herself including her website and all the paperwork.

Melissa said to me, "I have to test my skills about business since I went to school for business." She started with the money that was leftover when we were giving her an allowance. From the budget for her education, she had $6,000 left, though we told her to buy a car.

"I want to open my own business first," she said.

"You do want you want," we told her.

She goes to work Monday through Friday, and on the weekends, she works on her business, posting videos and pictures and modeling her clothes. It is going quite well.

Harley is very smart, but they cannot be opposites in personality. Melissa is a real go-getter and is committed to knowing what she wants to do. Harley likes to take his time and does what he wants. He will figure out what he wants for his life.

All the sacrifices it took to raise these two amazing children were, and are, worth it. When Harley went to school, we had to drive five hours north, while Melissa's drive to school was in the complete opposite direction, six hours south. Even though it was hard at times, we could not be prouder of both.

MY CAREER PATH

Even though I started out working as a Clinical Nursing Assistant (CNA), when I was in high school back home, I always had a teaching career in mind. My high school diploma was focused on teaching, but when I came to the United States, life was challenging, to say the least. In order to take care of my family, I had to change my career path, and the easiest way to do that was to become a CNA. It was something I did to survive.

While working at the nursing home, I went back to school and one day, I was reading the local newspaper and found out that the Regional Occupation Program (ROP) was looking for people to enlist in a program helping other people register for classes, something I was very interested in learning more about. The classes that they were registering people for were occupational life skills classes including a banking and finance class. Since I was interested in taking that class, I went to the center and registered as a student.

After the semester ended and I had completed that class, I was offered an internship at the local bank as a customer service representative, a position I enjoyed most of the time. While working at the bank, I learned more about finances and investing, especially about savings bonds. I learned about savings bonds when, one day, a lady customer came into the bank to buy savings bonds for her young grandkids.

Around Christmastime, she came up to my desk with a completed form, handed it to me, and said, "I want to buy savings bonds."

"One moment," I said to her and went to see my manager.

When he looked at the form, he said, "Oh - this is a savings bond form" and he showed me how to do it.

I went back to my desk, did the transaction, and asked her, "Why do you buy savings bonds for grandkids?"

"I don't buy toys – I buy them savings bonds. It is an investment for them," she replied.

When I went home, I told Mathias and the family about buying savings bonds, and from that point on, we started them for our kids. Every month, we would go to the bank together and complete the form; even though they were very young, I wanted to teach them about saving money early on. By the time they went to college, they had a lot of money saved.

There were times when we would give them money, and Harley, my son, would ask me, "Why does it have to go to the bank? Why can't I keep it and go buy something at the store?" At first, they didn't understand that we were doing this as an investment for them, but every time we got paid, we would go to the bank and buy savings bonds. Once, after Harley was much older, he called home asking for $500 to pay his rent. I told him, "You need to go to the bank. You have your savings bonds."

Harley did just that. He was so happy when he went to the bank and said, "This is so great. Now I know the meaning of buying savings bonds." They will do the same thing as soon as they have their own babies. I am grateful for the day that lady came into the bank to purchase savings bonds for her grandchildren. Otherwise, I probably would not have learned about them. Working at the bank was certainly an eye-opening experience, especially when it came to learning about money.

After two years of working at the bank, I discovered a new opportunity at the Social Security Administration's (SSA) Telecenter office in Salinas that was paying more money and offered better benefits. I applied and was hired right away as a customer service representative and worked there for two years. At the time, I didn't know that if you work at a bank, it is easy to get hired at SSA because they use almost the same systems and you know more about a person's finances so that experience working at the bank helped me get the job. Later, I found out that most of my colleagues came from banks.

However, it was my first time working in a cubicle, which was quite different because I was alone in this small area and talked to people I could not see. At the SSA, we answered questions about retirement, disability, and survivor benefits, and I learned quite a bit. For example, your retirement check can be garnished if you don't pay off your student loan. Also, those who turn 65 years old will be penalized if they don't apply for Medicare. The 800 number served all 50 states and even outside the country because those who retired and lived elsewhere could still call the SSA.

When I answered the phone with my accent, people would immediately ask me, "Are you in the U.S.?"

"Yes," was always my reply.

"You have a nice accent," he or she would say.

Sometimes, I had a hard time understanding them, and since SSA dealt with confidential information, people were always concerned about sharing it. Most of the time, I had to explain myself, saying that I live in California and English is my second language. After giving them some reassurance, they felt better and soon realized they were talking to an American.

Many times, I would say, "You have to be a U.S. Citizen to work for the SSA."

I enjoyed working with people who were vulnerable, disabled, or who were survivors like me, which taught me more about how to not rely on social security paychecks. It is not enough to live on, so you need a 401K or some other income source to handle retirement expenses.

Monterey County Office of Education

After working at the SSA for two years, I found a teaching job at Monterey County Office of Education as an Instructional Paraprofessional in the Department of Special Education in 2011. Right away, I was so happy because I finally found my dream job, even though I was a teacher's aide, ensuring the students were doing their work.

After four years, another opportunity arose when they were looking for more teachers to work for a school. Immediately, I applied and was selected to go to school in one of the universities in our area. As I write this book, I am taking classes at the local community college to become a teacher and get my teaching degree in education while still going to work. You have to be working in order to get the money to go to school, so I go to work during the day and attend school in the evening.

At this point, I have completed 40 credits, taking one or two classes per semester at Hartnell Community College, and have 20 more credits to finish before I can transfer to a 4-year college at California State University in Monterey Bay. Some of the classes I have taken include the following:

- Early Childhood Education
- Classes on Principles and Practice
- Child Growth and Development
- Introduction to Curriculum
- Child Family School and Community Relations
- Health, Sex, and Nutrition
- Teaching in Diverse Society
- Other general education classes

Even though I really like most of my classes, especially early childhood education, which is very informative, in most cases, I am the oldest one in the classroom. Most of the students are fresh out of high school and wonder what I am doing in school. When asked, I will tell them, "I am finishing my college education and have a daughter older than you."

"Really?" they say, surprised, "You look just like Mom!"

After graduating high school, I went to business school and now I am changing to teaching school, so they didn't transfer most of my business classes. I had to start fresh all over again and it took 10 years in between from when I graduated in 2003 to when I started again. Everything was hard for me because I had to adjust to going to school again, learn to take classes online, and find myself in a classroom with students of my children's age or younger.

It has been an adjustment, but I learn a lot from them, especially when I have to take classes online or in the classroom.

Hearing their stories is fascinating; when things are challenging for me on the computer, they help me. However, I help them by sharing my life experiences. In other words, we learn from each other.

For all those years, I didn't go to school; it was because I had to let our kids go so I could be there for them. Everyone went to school except me, and everyone in our family has a master's degree, but I do not. As a mom, I sacrificed myself for them, but it is now my turn to go back to school, and I have no regrets. It is actually a good thing because whenever I get stuck with homework, they can help me. The other day, Melissa was telling me how much she appreciated me and said, "You didn't finish getting your bachelor's degree so we could finish our school first." It has been important for me to be a good role model, and she really appreciates what we both did for her to go to school. Now, it is my turn.

As I mentioned earlier, I go to work in the day and attend school in the evening. In order for my work to pay for my scholarship, I have to show that I don't go to school at the same time I go to work. I have to show that I work Monday through Friday from 8 am – 3 pm and then go to school from 6 pm – 9 pm, three days a week, and some semesters, I go two days a week. It's not easy, but this is how I have to do it. My family keeps me motivated to keep going by helping with chores around the house, so I have more time to study.

Melissa lives at home and works remotely, and we don't know when they will be called back to work. It is nice having her home and learning from both her and Harley about all this new technology. Especially when doing my homework online, I don't know what I would do without them.

The other day, I had school homework that involved making a meal for children 3-6 years of age to teach them how to prepare a meal. It had to be a very easy meal preparation and make a video about it. Fortunately, Melissa was there to help me make the video as I demonstrated how to make a healthy Montebello Salad. I came up with that name because that is the area where we live. Here are the ingredients:

- Fresh spinach
- Cherry tomatoes
- Beets (cooked)
- Dried cranberries
- Croutons

Tossing all the ingredients with a balsamic vinaigrette was really good.

Working with Children with Special Needs

I always wanted to work with children, especially children with special needs. Although it is enjoyable, it has its own challenges. The program is for autistic kids who have a hard time understanding normal language because most of them don't speak. They are not deaf, but they don't speak. Autism is a developmental disorder characterized by difficulties with social interaction and communication and by restricted and repetitive behavior. Parents often notice signs during the first three years of their child's life. Autism is a brain-based developmental condition. Autistic children have communication difficulties, narrow interests, and repetitive behavior. Signs of autism might be noticeable in infancy or early childhood and might include a lack of interest in other people, including a lack of eye contact.

You have to be patient and have a routine for them. The most challenging days are Mondays because they are home over the weekend on Saturday and Sunday. When Monday morning rolls around, it is hard to start their routine all over again. It doesn't matter what break we take, whether over the weekend or a holiday, we have to teach them the routine repeatedly.

The other difficulty is that they don't communicate with us so if something happened at home, and it doesn't get communicated to the teacher, we don't understand why they might be behaving a certain way. Most of the autistic children I teach don't speak, and therefore, I have to make every effort to understand them with whatever behavior they are showing. Sometimes, they need more sleep, so we give them time to sleep at school, if needed, or time to cool down so they can accept our instructions.

Helping kids is something I enjoy doing, and because I know and understand they have so many challenges in life already, I want to make it easier for them. This year, I am teaching 4 – 6-year-old children with special education, but it is very hard to have a full classroom with only one aide. For normal education, they go to the school in the district with separate classrooms, and every child has their own curriculum based on their needs. Some are okay and score low to high; some can read – some do sounds, while some don't speak at all.

Some kids need more help than others, according to their level, while others can help themselves. Most of the kids come from divorced families, and very often, the father is not in the picture. Mom and grandma take care of the kids, which is another challenge of living without a dad. We have to be sensitive about that and understanding for the sake of the children.

With the COVID-19 pandemic, we had to do ZOOM classes, which were even harder for them to deal with. When the pandemic hit, the school was stopped altogether, so they were left at home, and their parents had to deal with them all day. When we resumed classes again, they didn't understand what was happening, especially because their routine was so off. We had to work so hard to get them back into a routine using ZOOM. Usually, we are right next to them to help them, which was easier, but that was next to impossible over ZOOM. In spite of all these challenges, teaching autistic children is still my passion and I am grateful for the opportunities to teach these very special children.

BECOMING A U.S. CITIZEN

When we came to the United States in late 2000, it was already challenging to become a U.S. citizen. Since 9/11, it became even more difficult because they seized everything, and we were afraid that we would not be given U.S. citizenship. Since September 11, 2001, the decade has seen a remarkable transformation of U.S. immigration law and policy. In the aftermath of the 9/11 attacks, as concerns grew about a possible terrorist presence in the United States, the federal government—along with many in the public at large—linked immigration screening and enforcement to the protection of national security. Consequently, lawmakers, federal agencies that engage with immigrants, and the courts that adjudicate immigration matters began to adapt their roles and responsibilities to meet the objectives of the War on Terror. https://www.americanbar.org/groups/crsj/publications/human_rights_magazine_home/human_rights_vol38_2011/human_rights_winter2011/9-11_transformation_of_us_immigration_law_policy/

During the last ten years, an emphasis on national security has made its way into U.S. immigration laws, policies, and agencies. Border areas and ports of entry are now framed as potential sources of vulnerability, and the federal government has increased its oversight of noncitizens who seek to enter the United States, imposing restrictions on arriving aliens, including asylum seekers. The federal government has also used immigration systems and policies as broad nets designed to catch persons who might engage in terrorist activities, whether now or at some point in the future.

In addition, the federal government has expanded the definition of "terrorist activity" to include a broad spectrum of conduct. In so doing, noncitizens who stumble into this controversial designation lose access to important immigration benefits. The responses by the federal government to 9/11 have led to an unprecedented increase in detentions, deportations, and confusion within immigrant communities.

The remarkable changes within the immigration system seemed to occur almost overnight and reflected the beginning of a pattern of utilizing immigration law and the country's immigration-related agencies to meet national security objectives. Fourteen months after the attacks, in November 2002, Congress enacted the Homeland Security Act (Pub. L. No. 107-296), which led to a significant overhaul of federal agencies. The law brought more than twenty federal agencies (such as the Immigration and Naturalization Service, formerly part of the U.S. Department of Justice (DOJ), as well as the Federal Emergency Management Agency, the Transportation Security Administration, and others) under the umbrella of the newly created U.S. Department of Homeland Security (DHS).

Congress created a new Cabinet-level position in the DHS secretary and defined the department's primary mission as preventing terrorism and minimizing the impact of terrorist attacks within the United States. The Immigration and Naturalization Service (INS) was separated into three components within DHS:

1. United States Citizenship and Immigration Services (USCIS)
2. Customs and Border Protection (CBP)
3. Immigration and Customs Enforcement (ICE)

While these structural changes were being made, many interim rules and regulations were instituted that would have a significant impact on immigrants, particularly those from MASA communities. Within weeks after the 9/11 attacks, Congress and the DOJ had made decisions to alter the authority and scope of federal agencies. For example, the DOJ issued a regulation that enabled the detention of noncitizens for forty-eight hours or longer in the event of "an emergency or other extraordinary circumstances" without making any charging determinations. (Custody Procedures, 66 Fed. Reg. 48331 (Sept. 20, 2001)).

A defining feature of post-9/11 immigration policy has been the heightened scrutiny of those who seek to enter the United States. Soon after 9/11, the federal government tightened the process of issuing temporary visas to tourists, business visitors, students, and other foreign nationals. Specifically, through provisions in the Enhanced Border Security and Visa Reform Act of 2002 (Pub. L. No. 107-103) and the Homeland Security Act, the government called for machine-readable, tamper-proof visas; enhanced use of technology and data-sharing between agencies;

training of consular officers on fraud terrorist identification; additional requirements for student visas; and more.

As a result of these reforms, prospective students, business visitors, and others—often from countries perceived to be sources of terrorist threats—were denied entry to the United States. Universities and business groups criticized the restrictions on visa issuance, arguing that the United States might lose intellectual and entrepreneurial capital to countries with more permissive entry requirements. As an empirical matter, nonimmigrant admissions noticeably dropped in 2002 and 2003 but have increased across most visa categories since 2004. (DHS Yearbook of Immigration Statistics: 2009.)

Coming here as refugees, we had an advantage because most of our legal paperwork was done in the refugee camp. They did all of our background checks while we were there, making sure we didn't have any criminal records, and no issues with the government back where we came from because the US does not want to bring anyone into the country who could be a potential criminal. We went through that whole process, including a health checkup to make sure we did not have any infectious disease. Once everything was cleared, then we could leave.

We were given a one-time travel document from the U.S. Embassy; it was not a passport, but it allowed us to come into the country. This was a good thing because we received our work permit and green card once we were here. Soon after that, we received our Social Security number and were able to apply for our ID. Even though we had all those documents, we were still fearful that the 9/11 situation would affect our lives.

In order to become a U.S. citizen, you have to be here at least five years before you can start applying for U.S. citizenship. We applied as a family for our citizenship but since the children were minors, only parents could apply. Once parents are U.S. citizens, then the children automatically become citizens, so Melissa and Harley did not have to apply. Since our niece, Cheka, was not our biological child, she had to apply on her own and had to wait until she was 18 years old – you have to be an adult.

Before applying for citizenship, we had to learn all about the United States, its history, political climate, and learn the language, English. There were 100 questions on the study exam all about the U.S. constitution and policies. We were told that when we take the test, we would be asked 20 questions out of the 100 questions and were required to pass 18 questions to become a U.S. citizen. You must pass the exam to get U.S. citizenship. We passed our test with flying colors, getting all the questions right, and became U.S. citizens in 2005. We felt so good when we became US citizens; we were free and American.

With 9/11 happening, it reminded us about the war back home, and since we had run away from a war, we couldn't help but think, here we were in another country with more horrible events happening. It brought back that terrible memory of what was going on back home.

Regardless of those dreadful memories of war, I remember the day the officer gave us the certificate of U.S. citizenship.

He said to us, "I know that all of you will do well. Now you are American, and when people bring up your accent, the best answer you can give is, 'Yes - I have an accent because I speak more than one language.'

Those words have always stayed with me, but I felt free. Every time someone mentions our accent, in some ways, it reminds me that we are not American, but when that immigration officer told us what to say, he made us feel that we were smarter than someone else who only speaks one language. People make comments about our accents all the time.

When I don't open my mouth, most people think we are simply African American but as soon as they notice our accent, they ask, "Where are you from?"

"I am from the Democratic Republic of Congo," I always say. I am proud of that because that is me and my history. I value what we had back home, and I am also proud of being American.

For our children, they don't feel 100% Congolese or 100% Black Americans. At school, especially in college, they have African Americans in their classes, and, of course, they want to join them in conversation because they are Blacks, but when they do, they don't feel like they belong. Why? Because many of the African Americans in their classes want to them to act like African Americans. They don't feel like they belong if they don't act a certain way or like them.

When we are in Africa, we don't feel like an outsider, but living here in the United States and seeing other African Americans on television, they don't have an accent, speak English and look at us as African Americans until they read our last name, and then immediately say, "You are not from here."

We have never experienced prejudice in our lives as a refugee. Back home in Africa, everyone is black: teachers, nurses, ministers, etc. in the country. When we went to school, there was no talk about 'you can't be president because you are Black.' You think you can be anything you want to be as long as you go to school. We always thought to ourselves, "I can become somebody." This is something we have taught our children from a young age and engrained in them that if they study and work hard, they can be whatever they want to be.

Since coming to the United States, we have found that many people think that people from Africa could be better and smart based on what they have seen on television. However, it doesn't matter what you see on television or the fact that I come from a rich family; there will always be poor and rich people in every country around the world. People need to be educated about Africa and its beautiful cities. Still, it appears that the media only shows the bad side of the country or videos of homeless people. There are homeless people in the U.S., Europe, Africa, Asia, and many places throughout the world – that is just the reality.

My Parents Come to Visit

When my dad and mom came to visit us from Africa, we sponsored my parents and did all the paperwork required to become permanent US residents if they wanted to live here. We started this process after we had received our citizenship and bought our first house. It took two years to do all the paperwork, beginning in 2005, and since we were more financially stable, we wanted to do something for our parents. At the end of the application process, we had to do a DNA test to make sure they were my parents in order for them to be admitted into the country. It took two months to get the results back, and they were a 99.9% match.

After my parents got their visas to visit the U.S., they finally arrived. We were so happy to show them around and took them to all sorts of places, including Costco, as we thought they would get a kick out of seeing such a huge place to shop. Outside the entrance, we saw a homeless guy asking for help.

He was looking at my Dad who said, "This person wants us to help him – the writing on his sign says, "I need help."

"I know," I replied.

My Dad looked at him and said, "Here in America – I am shocked to see someone asking for help."

"Yes – remember dad – there are rich and poor people everywhere we go."

"In Africa, people would help him. America should help him," he insisted.

"No Dad, that is back home. Not here," I said emphatically.

"He is White – why can't the white people help him?" he said, still not convinced. "We see White people from the USA going to Africa to help people there. Why is this guy on the street begging? Why can't someone help him?" he asked again.

Back home in Africa, we didn't have homeless people on the street because we are family-oriented – there is always someone who will help those who need it. They would not let people go on the streets and beg.

My Dad was confused and didn't understand why and said, "This is America? All this Begging? No one can help him?"

It was so hard for him to understand and with my efforts to explain everything; both my parents were still in shock.

"How could this happen?" my Dad asked again. "The image we have of the USA is one of beauty." When he saw all the homeless on the street, he said to me, "I really appreciate you doing what you did because if an American can live on the street and you came from Africa with nothing – you must be working so hard."

That was when my Dad realized that we deserved this new life. When they came for a visit, I took one week off to be with them, but Mathias continued to work, and the kids went to school.

After three days of them living with us, my Dad asked, "Why do you have to go to work every day?"

"I have to work and help my husband pay the bills," I replied.

Since he has six wives and twenty-two kids, he supports everyone. In his mindset, he said, "Women don't work. It is up to the husband to provide for the entire family."

"Dad – things are different here than back home," I replied. "I have to work to help my husband and kids."

"Your husband can't provide for you all? You don't have enough money to support you and your children?" he asked in shock.

"No – I have to help," I said.

"Can't you just work 2-3 days a week?" he asked with eyebrows raised.

"No – then I have to come home and start cooking," I replied.

Even though he had all those wives back home, he still had maids to do the housework.

He could not understand why I had to work so much and then come home to cook. He looked at me and asked, "Why don't you hire a maid and have someone else cook meals for you?"

"No, dad," I replied. "We can't afford a maid."

He was surprised and said, "You are working too much."

My dad stayed for three months and then went back home, but my mom stayed in the U.S. for seven years altogether. She stayed with us for about two years but was rather annoyed that I didn't have a small baby for her to take care of. Begging me to have another baby so she could be busy for a while, I said, "No."

In the meantime, my brother immigrated to the U.S. with his wife, who was pregnant, so we sent my mom to my brother's home so she could help take care of the baby. She stayed there for five years until it was time for the child to start school, then she went back home. When my mom looks back on her time here, she finds it rather limiting or confining because she didn't speak English, rarely saw any neighbors, and was often stuck in the house day and night. She found it odd that we told her to keep the doors locked throughout the day even though she was there. Back home in Africa, the doors are never locked; the front door is open all day. We only closed it before going to bed.

Eventually, my dad encouraged her to come home, but when my mom went back, she was like an American, and my dad saw a big change in her. He said, "You sent me someone else – that is not my wife." My dad was expecting an obedient wife without talking back to him. When my dad had gone back home after being here for three months, he built a huge, 4-story house. When my mom arrived home, she first asked him, "Where is the closet?"

"What is a closet?" my dad asked her puzzled.

My Mom replied, "Where should I put my clothes?"

I built this big house, and all you can say is, "Where is the closet?"

My mom had become Americanized, and my dad was not happy about that. From that point on, things between them could have been better. It took them at least six months to adjust to each other again. To keep the peace, she tried to do her best to accommodate his wishes.

When my Dad came here to visit us, he wanted to see a White doctor and do all his check-ups while he was in America to make sure everything was okay, healthwise. He knew that we had all the latest technology in the U.S., and he wanted to take advantage of that, but he didn't speak English. Mathias had to go with him to translate for him, but this turned out to be a good thing because he apologized to Mathias for not wanting him to marry his daughter.

"I am really sorry about what happened," he said. Now that we are here in America, if you hadn't married my daughter, I don't know where she would have ended up. I am happy now that you did marry her.

Mathias said, "I accept your apology – you were just doing your job as a parent. Even when I think about someone wanting to marry Melissa, I realize you were protecting your daughter, and I would do the same. You didn't know that I would be a good husband. I do understand."

From that point on, they were friends. We were happy that he came to that conclusion and very glad that he apologized to Mathias.

UPS AND DOWNS
OF MARRIAGE

I have been married for a long time, 26 years to be exact as I write this book, and I have enjoyed it for the most part. When you are young and in love, everything is all rosy and joyous. However, five years into our marriage, when we were in the refugee camp, I started having some issues surrounding our niece.

I was very young and didn't understand my husband's thought process well, so I asked him, "What are we going to do about Cheka, our niece? What are we going to do for the interview to get to the US? Since she is not legally our child, she may not be able to go with us—what are we going to do with her? Are we going to claim her as our niece?"

Mathias said, "No – we will claim her as our own child because she may not be allowed into the country if we claim her as our niece."

Both of us were trying to decide without the correct information, and Mathias wanted to protect her, especially since the war was going on back home. I was not comfortable with claiming her as our own kid because, at my age, it was obvious I was too young to be her Mom.

Then Mathias said, "I will claim I had her before I married you."

Well, that didn't go well with me at all, and I said, "No – if we do that, it will be in writing on paper, and I don't want to put that lie on paper."

"What do you want to do? We can't leave her here, he said. "The war is still going on – no one is home."

"Why can't we claim her as our niece?" I asked.

Mathias said, "No – if we don't claim her as our own child, they won't accept her. They will think that we took her or something."

"We need to claim her as our niece," I insisted. "We need to tell the truth. I don't want to lie. She is not our child. We don't know the laws, and if we have a problem when we arrive in the U.S., that will bring more issues to us. Let's say she is our niece."

Eventually, when the time came, we claimed her as our niece in the interview and explained how we ended up with her. We were honest and told them what happened, how she had come to visit us for her summer vacation, and she was with us when we were suddenly attacked.

Fortunately, the person interviewing us understood that and said, "Since she is not your biological child, we will file two separate files—one for your family and the other for your niece. You will still be a family, but since she is a minor, you will be the guardian for her."

So, that is how we came to the U.S. as a family with our own file, and she had her own separate file. Once we arrived in the U.S., we were able to get all the documents required to start working, and our lives began.

However, Mathias felt uncomfortable coming to the U.S. without declaring her as our child. She kept asking us if she did something wrong, which, of course, she didn't do anything wrong. When I tried to talk to him about her, he would always say, "You need to deal with her. You don't always have to tell me what is going on with her."

I didn't like his response, saying, "We need to educate her as a family, not just leave it all up to me."

I didn't understand his thought process, and he didn't like how I insisted she come to the U.S. as our niece instead of our child. In my mind, I was afraid and didn't think I would be living with her for the rest of her life when we had to flee the country. In the long run, I had to adjust my mind and realize that I would have to be a mom for this child. It took me some time to figure that out. At times, it was a struggle. One day before I went to work, I told my niece that I would like her to do the dishes so that I could start cooking right away when I got home from work. She didn't do it, and I was so upset with her.

I told Mathias, "She has to wash the dishes when I ask her to do it."

Mathias said to me, "I am tired of you telling me about her. You need to deal with her."

When things like that happened, I was so unhappy about it. Whenever I tried to educate my niece, she felt I didn't love her. Mathias loved her, but that created resentment toward me. He thought I didn't like her because I didn't want her to come with us, but that was a huge misunderstanding.

From that point on, our married life was not so good. We didn't love each other like before, which was so painful for me. It took me a long time, actually 10 years, to get over it. Even though

Mathias knew I was on his side, he still felt like I didn't like his family members.

My thoughts turned to the time when my whole family didn't want me to marry Mathias, and those thoughts kept coming to mind.

Both of us knew something was wrong between us and we finally sat down to discuss our marriage.

I said to Mathias, "This is too much for us to deal with on our own. We need to go to a marriage counselor."

Initially, he resisted and said, "No."

"We need to read books about problems with marriages," I replied.

At least, he agreed to read books and said, "Yes."

I went online to research books on fixing marriages and found three books that we read together that really did help us. However, there was a lot more to our situation than I realized and

we finally went to a marriage counselor. Mathias finally realized that he was hurting me so badly and our marriage was not turning out the way either one of us thought it would be. Plus, I wanted to know and understand why he was acting the way he was and why this was happening.

Our niece, Cheka, was innocent of all of this, and it was simply a misunderstanding between Mathias and me. We wanted our children to know this because they both realized something was wrong between us. After finishing the marriage counseling, we continued reading the books, did the assignments that the counselor gave us, and added the knowledge that we took from the books we read, which included "*His Needs Her Needs*" and "*Love Busters*" by Willard Harley. We liked his last name – LOL.

After reading these books, I finally understood why I was feeling what I was feeling. Though it was difficult to put into words, I also understood why he was acting the way he was. After reading both books, he understood himself better, and this brought a lot of change to our relationship. From then on, we understood each other better and what life means as a married couple. We also thought about when you say "I love you" – what does that mean? You can say those three little words hundreds of times, but if you don't act lovingly, then you are not loving.

Mathias said, "I didn't know I was doing this to you."

"You have to be practical," I replied. "That means washing the dishes, helping me clean the house, and making the bed – that is how we can show love to each other. You can't just say 'I love you' and then hurt me."

We had gone through ten years of suffering, and I finally said, "Enough is enough. We have to do something if we are going to be together. We have to change, and it has to be a big change."

He did apologize to me and said, "I didn't realize I was hurting you."

Knowing he was on my side, I accepted his apology and said, "You need to change and understand that you are the only one I chose to be with. If not, our children will suffer if we do divorce."

"I understand that," he replied.

Mathias loves me dearly and we do everything together. As a result of us reading Willard Harley's books and going to a marriage counselor, he understands me more, and I understand him more. These two books really changed our lives. Now, we are in a good place, loving each other and making decisions together, especially when it comes to financial issues. We make a point of sitting down and talking about things and making sure that what we are doing is beneficial for us both. Now we go to bed happy, whereas before, it was more like "Don't touch me."

The last chapter in the *Love Busters* book really helped us the most. At the beginning of the chapter, the author, Willard, talks about the importance of having a love bank. The concept is rather simple; when two people meet, they create an account, and every time you do something good for your spouse, you are depositing love into your account. When you do something bad to your spouse, you are withdrawing love. That concept really helped us see and understand why we had an estrangement from each other. Every time I asked him something, he didn't respond the way I wanted or needed, so he withdrew love from me. When he does something I like, he is depositing love in the love bank.

When we understood that concept, we made an effort to make more deposits versus withdrawals. We continue to use that concept to this day. If I do something he doesn't like, we are able to realize its consequences. We make sure we go to bed in a good place. Before I used to keep it in my heart, not say anything, and just be mad at him, but he wouldn't understand what was happening. It would be so uncomfortable in our house, like walking on eggshells.

Using the love bank helped us a lot. For example, we ask questions of each other like, "How did I do today? Did I listen to you today?" If there were any moments he did not listen to me, or I was not happy about something, then he would apologize and say something like, "I didn't realize that bothered you." Once he apologized – we would both feel better. That system we created helped us then and still helps us today, and we are confident it will continue to help us in the future.

After reading both of Willard Harley's books, we were doing better, but we realized that we still needed to go to marriage counseling. I really needed someone professional telling us what is going on in our relationship. We went to a marriage counselor for six months once a month for an hour. Having to pay for the session every time, the cost of doing that actually brought us together – we needed to do our best so we wouldn't have to keep paying that high fee. The cost helped us to reconcile because we both knew we weren't getting anywhere alone. All I could think of was if we divorced, who would take care of our children? We both realized that the kids would suffer the most. Since we didn't have any family in the U.S., there was no place for them to go, so we needed to figure something out and work on our marriage, which we did happily.

WHAT THE FUTURE HOLDS

10

Being together and seeing our grandkids while we are still young enough to enjoy them is our dream. Since we worked so hard for everything we have, we are more in love today than ever before - we understand each other and do everything together. The turning point was our children because by that time if we were not together, we knew our children would suffer, and we both understood that reality. However, they didn't know what was going on at the time this was happening.

Now, we take time each day to talk to each other and we started that ritual every week on Saturday, determined to make time for us. One thing that was missing in our life that revolved around that concept of making time for us was "Date Night." We were so busy with life, coming home from work, cooking, and taking care of our children, but all that time, we never took time for ourselves or sat down and talked about our own problems. We didn't have that time.

Now, every Saturday, after dinner, we sit down together, sometimes in the dining room or bedroom, and we are both open to ask any questions. We have to answer the questions honestly and be sincere, something we didn't do before. We would also take time to read the books together, identify the problem(s) according to the examples in the book, and do a self-assessment. From there, we understood what was going on with each of us. When we understood that, we were able to redeem ourselves and make an effort not to make that same mistake.

We bought a box of cards with questions on it, and every date night, we sat down and asked each other questions, which helped us to understand each other. Here are 3 examples of the questions we ask each other:

- How do we complement each other, and how has that changed over time?
- Who has played the biggest role in our relationship that isn't one of us? Why?
- Who has more power in our relationship and how has that changed?

Sometimes, we don't have an answer, but we ask it again and very often are more prepared to answer it the following date night. We also figured out hobbies that we like to do together. For example, I like gardening, and before we started doing date nights, Mathias didn't know that I really liked gardening, so when we moved to our second house, I created a landscaping plan to make sure we could have a small garden.

I planted vegetables to grow, and one day, before I went to work, I asked Mathias, "Can you please water the garden?"

He said, "Yes."

When I came home from work, the first thing I did was checking the garden and realized he didn't do it and was rather upset.

As soon as I saw him, I said, "Before I left, I asked you to water the garden."

He explained to me, "I had to do something else. I will do it in the evening."

I wouldn't say I liked that answer at all, and I blew up. Everything that happened before came out, and he soon realized how angry I was at him. But he didn't understand why and asked, "Why are you so mad?"

I told him how upset I was a long time ago before we came to the U.S., and I was mad. He had no idea. To say the least, it was a miserable night that day. Before going to bed, he watered the garden, and that was the day he found out how much I liked gardening.

He said, "These are just weeds and grass. Why are you so mad? I told you I would get to it this evening."

"You don't understand – you can call it weeds or grass – to me, this is very important," I replied.

During the course of that day and night, what happened between us opened up a well of problems that had been kept deep inside. Mathias didn't realize how much I was hurting, but when we opened up that wound, everyone and everything became clear about what I like and don't like. And we did the same for him, too. In the end, I am glad he didn't water the garden, so we had the opportunity to talk everything out. It turned out that Mathias was unhappy, too, in how we were interacting, so it ended up being a good thing.

We have an apple and an orange tree in our backyard, and I would love to see the grandkids picking apples from the tree – that would make me so happy. It would be great to hear one of them say, "We want to see our grandparents and pick apples." We also bought a cherry tree and planted it to remind Mathias that this tree is for our grandchildren so they can come to our home and eat cherries. We see ourselves living here for a long time.

My Career

As far as my career goes, I am going to continue going to school so that one day, I will have my master's degree in education and be fully credentialed to be a special education teacher, teaching at the same place I am now. I don't see myself ever going back to Africa to live other than to visit. We have no desire to retire there because I do not want to miss being with my grandchildren. I want to be here so I can spend time with them.

Other Dreams

I also see myself and Mathias traveling the world and going on romantic vacations. We have talked about going to Australia, which has beautiful landscaping that we would really like to see. Asia, especially South Korea, is another place we would like to visit because we like to drive Korean cars like the Kia and Hyundai. It would be fun to go see where the cars are made. Hawaii is another dream vacation destination because the tropical climate is similar to Africa, and the food is delicious.

Another dream of mine is to create a non-profit in education back home, in Africa, by opening libraries and building schools for low-income kids. The non-profit would also help pay their tuition, school supplies, and uniforms so they can go to school. Our family has always valued education, and we would be more than happy to help children in Africa get an education. This would be a huge undertaking but something I feel very passionate about in this world.

We have not been back to Africa mainly because we have been so busy with our children to ensure they were supported. Now that they are grown, it would be easier for us to go, but it is costly to go to Africa. We wanted to use the money we had for their education. Since they have finished with school, we can save some money and use it to return to Africa one day in the near future. We want to check on our parents and relatives and look into starting the non-profit through fundraising and using our own money. We have already started building funds for that project.

It has always been hard to communicate with our family in the Democratic Republic of Congo because we had to buy a calling card that only gives us 20 minutes, and we spent a lot of money to put their number on that card. However, every minute, the time would decrease because sometimes, when we would call, it would ring, and someone would pick up and say hello, but then we wouldn't hear them anymore. We kept waiting to hear them again but then nothing would happen, and soon, the money on the card was gone. Even though we would stop the call, we would have only $10 left on the card, which was not a lot of time. Sometimes, we would buy $100 worth of cards and find the person to talk to but end up yelling because we couldn't understand each other. By the time we could tell what we wanted to tell them, we were on our 4th card.

Today, it is much easier with cell phones, and we also use free Whatsapp, but you have to talk with someone who also has that app. If they go near a cellphone tower, they can talk for free, and it makes it much easier to communicate at home.

As far as my parents were living in the U.S., my dad could have stayed, but he was bored and stayed inside all the time. Also, he didn't speak the language, and he is a businessman, so he went back home to Africa to continue with his business as usual. As far as we are concerned, we want to live happily ever after, focus on school, get my degree, and do the job I love—teaching special education.

ABOUT THE AUTHOR

Author, Para-Educator, Wife, and Mother of two children, Bitisho has lived a life many people cannot begin to imagine. Fleeing her country, the Democratic Republic of Congo, Bitisho arrived in the United States with her husband, three children, the clothes on their back and $100. Through incredible determination, grit, and strength of character, Bitisho built a new life with her husband and family, which is evident throughout her true story.

An advocate of education, Bitisho plans to start an education program in Africa, build libraries and schools for low-income students, and help them get an education. When she is not working with special education students, she looks forward to having a house full of grandchildren and a large garden and continuing to enjoy life in the United States.

For more information, write to Bitisho at myjourneytoanewworld@gmail.com